J. K. Rowling

My Favorite Writer

Bryan Pezzi

WEIGL PUBLISHERS INC.

Published by Weigl Publishers Inc.
350 5th Avenue, Suite 3304, PMB 6G
New York, NY 10118-0069
USA
Web site: www.weigl.com

Library of Congress Cataloging-in-Publication Data

Pezzi, Bryan.
  J.K. Rowling / Bryan Pezzi.
      p. cm. -- (My favorite writer)
  Includes index.
  ISBN 1-59036-287-X (hard cover : alk. paper) -- ISBN 1-59036-293-4
(soft cover : alk. paper)
  1. Rowling, J. K.--Juvenile literature. 2. Authors, English--20th century-
-Biography--Juvenile literature. 3. Potter, Harry (Fictitious character)--
Juvenile literature. 4. Creative writing--Juvenile literature. I. Title. II.
Series.
  PR6068.O93Z825 2005
  823'.914--dc22

                                                    2004029929

Project Coordinator
Tina Schwartzenberger

Substantive Editor
Frances Purslow

Design
Terry Paulhus

Layout
Jeff Brown

Photo Researchers
Jason Novak
Kim Winiski

Printed in the United States of America
1 2 3 4 5 6 7 8 9 10 09 08 07 06 05

Contents

J. K. Rowling

MILESTONES

1965 Born on July 31 in Chipping Sodbury, Great Britain

1987 Graduates from the University of Exeter, where she studied French and **Classics**

1990 Moves to Manchester, England, and begins writing

1991 Moves to Oporto, Portugal, to teach English

1994 Moves to Edinburgh, Scotland

1995 Completes her first novel and hires a literary **agent**

1997 *Harry Potter and the Philosopher's Stone* is published in Britain

1998 *Harry Potter and the Philosopher's Stone* is published in the United States with the title *Harry Potter and the Sorcerer's Stone*

2000 *Harry Potter and the Goblet of Fire* becomes the fastest-selling book in history

2001 First Harry Potter movie appears in cinemas

Joanne Kathleen (J. K.) Rowling has brought magic to millions of people. In the mid-1990s, she was a single mother struggling to publish her first novel. Today, she is a celebrity with fans around the world. The adventures of Harry Potter, a young boy with round glasses and a lightning-bolt scar on his forehead, have made her famous.

Harry Potter appeared in 1997 when Joanne's first novel, *Harry Potter and the Philosopher's Stone*, was published in Great Britain. The book tells the story of an orphan named Harry, who does not know he is a wizard. Harry discovers a world of magic and wonder when he attends Hogwarts School. There, he studies magic with his new friends, Ron Weasley and Hermione Granger. No other children's writer has achieved the same success as Joanne. More than a quarter of a billion Harry Potter books have been sold worldwide. Translated into 61 languages, the books are sold in more than 200 countries.

Early Childhood

Joanne Rowling was born on July 31, 1965. Joanne's father, Peter, was an engineer, and her mother, Anne, was a **lab technician**. In 1967, Joanne's sister, Diana, was born. The family lived in the town of Chipping Sodbury in western England. When Joanne was 4 years old, the family moved to Winterbourne. Winterbourne is near Bristol in southwestern England.

As a young girl, Joanne was known as "Jo" to her family. Diana was called "Di." Joanne was short and round, and wore very thick glasses. She was the "bright one" in the family, while her sister Di was the "pretty one." Neither girl liked these labels. Joanne was bossy with her sister, but she was shy with strangers. Joanne and her sister often argued.

Chipping Sodbury is an old market town that was founded in the middle of the twelfth century.

Although they fought, Joanne and Di were best friends. They enjoyed playing together. Joanne invented plays and skits, and Di acted in them. The girls never tired of these dramas. One of their favorite **scenarios** to act out was for one girl to cling to the other girl's hand, pretending she was dangling from a cliff. The girls were actually sitting at the top of the stairs. The dangling girl would pretend she was going to fall from a cliff, and would beg her sister to hold her. The scenario always ended with the dangling girl pretending to fall to her doom.

Joanne also enjoyed making up stories. Sometimes she invented tales to entertain her sister. Soon, she began writing her stories down on paper. Joanne wrote her first book when she was 6 years old. It was a story about a bunny named Rabbit. In her story, Rabbit caught **measles**. All of Rabbit's friends came to visit him. One of his friends was an insect named Miss Bee. Joanne was very proud of her first book.

Many children enjoy dressing up and acting for their families, friends, and neighbors.

Growing Up

Joanne liked the name Potter. She preferred it to her own name.

The village of Winterbourne, where Joanne lived between the ages of 4 and 9, is located on the outskirts of Bristol, England.

Joanne enjoyed school in Winterbourne, especially drawing and pottery. Joanne was happiest when she was reading and writing. After school, Joanne played with her sister or with friends. Sometimes she played with a brother and sister with the last name of Potter. Joanne liked the name Potter. She preferred it to her own name, Rowling, which is pronounced "rolling." This name lead to jokes like "Rowling stone" and "Rowling pin."

Around the time of her ninth birthday, Joanne's family moved to Tutshill, a small village in Wales. This was not a happy time for Joanne. Not only did she have to move to a new home, but her favorite grandparent, Kathleen, died. Joanne was very sad about the death of her grandmother. She later took her grandmother's name as her own middle name.

Joanne found it difficult to adjust to her new school. She did not like the school. On her first day of classes, Joanne failed a math test because she had not learned fractions. As punishment, her teacher sat her in the row reserved for students who did poorly. Joanne worked very hard to earn higher grades. By the end of the year, she was able to sit with the better students.

Joanne grew happier when she entered secondary school at 11 years of age. Here she met Sean Harris, who became one of her best friends. Sean supported Joanne's goal to be a writer.

Joanne says Sean was similar to the character of Ron Weasley in the Harry Potter books. Joanne was more like Hermione Granger. She was shy, bookish, and a worrywart. As teenagers, Joanne and Sean took rides in Sean's car. This was Joanne's first taste of freedom and her happiest teenage memory.

Inspired to Write

Some details in the Harry Potter books come from Joanne's childhood. She grew up in Tutshill, Wales. Tutshill has a castle, which sits on a hill overlooking the town. Joanne also lived next door to a cemetery. Castles and cemeteries are important **settings** in Joanne's books.

Chepstow Castle, near Tutshill, Wales, likely inspired some of the settings in Joanne's books.

When Joanne was 15, her mother, Anne, was diagnosed with multiple sclerosis (MS). This disease attacks the **central nervous system**. It can cause **paralysis** and blindness. Some people with MS experience periods of **remission**. Their disease may stop progressing or they may begin recovering for a while. Unfortunately, this did not happen for Joanne's mother. Her illness grew steadily worse. This was a difficult time for Joanne. It was hard for Joanne to watch her mother's health fail.

In 1983, Joanne graduated with honors from Wyedean Comprehensive School. She wanted to enroll in Oxford University, but she was not accepted. Instead, Joanne enrolled at the University of Exeter, on the southern coast of England. She studied French and Classics. The best part of Joanne's French education was spending a year in Paris, France.

While in Paris, Joanne worked as a teacher's assistant. In Paris, she saw many famous landmarks, including the Eiffel Tower.

After graduating from university, Joanne moved to London, United Kingdom. She worked as a secretary, but found that she did not enjoy **clerical** work much. Joanne said she was disorganized. She also found it difficult to pay attention in meetings. Instead of paying attention and taking detailed notes, Joanne often wrote story ideas. When no one was looking, she wrote stories on her computer. Joanne wanted to write. She found clerical work boring. Joanne also worked as a researcher for Amnesty International. Amnesty International is an organization that promotes and protects **human rights** around the world. Joanne worked at this job longer than any other.

In 2004, Joanne received an honorary degree from the University of Edinburgh. An honorary degree is given as an award. This means Joanne did not have to complete the usual requirements.

Favorite Authors

Joanne loved reading when she was young. Her mother, Anne, often read to her two young daughters. Then Joanne began reading books for herself. "I loved the library," Joanne says. As a child, she liked to read books by E. Nesbit, Paul Gallico, and C. S. Lewis. Her favorite book was *The Little White Horse* by Elizabeth Goudge. When she was 19, Joanne read J. R. R. Tolkien's fantasy series, *The Lord of the Rings*. As an adult, Joanne still finds time to read. Her favorite author is Jane Austen. This nineteenth-century British novelist wrote humorous and witty stories about love, marriage, and English society.

Learning the Craft

In 1990, Joanne moved to Manchester, England. On a crowded train from Manchester to London, the idea for Harry Potter first popped into her head. While the train was delayed, Joanne imagined a scrawny, black-haired boy with glasses. He had magical powers but did not know he was a wizard. Harry Potter grew more and more real to Joanne. She imagined Harry's lightning-bolt scar and Hogwarts School, along with many of Harry's teachers and classmates. Joanne did not have a pen and was too shy to ask to borrow one. She used her imagination and tried to remember the details so that she could write them down later.

That night, Joanne began writing her first Harry Potter novel. Over the next few months, the **manuscript** grew. Joanne also wrote down ideas for other books in the series.

That same year, something happened to greatly change Joanne's life. Her mother, Anne, died at the age of 45. It was a terrible time for Joanne, her sister, and their father. They never imagined that Anne would die so young. After this terrible event, Joanne was desperate to move away.

One day, Joanne's train from Manchester to London was delayed for 4 hours. She had plenty of time to imagine Harry Potter and his adventures.

Joanne moved to Portugal and found a job teaching English. She continued to work on her novel. The book changed after Joanne's mother died. Harry's feelings toward his dead parents became much deeper and more real. During Joanne's first weeks in Portugal, she wrote her favorite chapter of the book. It is called "The Mirror of Erised." In this chapter, Harry finds a magic mirror that reveals his deepest desire. Harry's greatest wish is to be with his parents.

While living in Portugal, Joanne married a Portuguese **journalist**. In 1993, Joanne gave birth to her daughter, Jessica. The marriage did not last. In 1994, Joanne returned to Great Britain with her young daughter. She had not finished writing her first novel.

Inspired to Write

Harry Potter's school, Hogwarts, is similar to the school that Joanne attended in Wales. While Joanne did not learn spells or potions, her school had four houses, just like Hogwarts. Students were ages 11 through 17, and they wore uniforms. Like the character of Hermione, Joanne achieved top marks and became **head girl** in her final year.

■ Joanne taught English in Oporto, or Porto, Portugal. Porto is Portugal's second-largest city.

Getting Published

When Joanne and her daughter left Portugal, they moved to Edinburgh, Scotland, where Joanne's sister was living. At first, life in Edinburgh was difficult for Joanne. She was a single parent living in poor conditions. Joanne applied for **welfare** to support herself and her daughter. Sometimes she found secretarial work for a few hours a week. Joanne intended to start teaching again, but this idea worried her. She did not think she would have time to finish her book if she taught school and cared for Jessica.

Joanne put all of her energy into finishing her novel. She worked on her book every evening. After Jessica fell asleep, Joanne wrote. During this time, she did all of her writing with a pen and paper. Joanne did not have a typewriter or a computer.

Finishing the book was difficult for Joanne. Sometimes she hated the book, and sometimes she became depressed. Still, Joanne had a good story and characters that she loved.

The Publishing Process

Publishing companies receive hundreds of manuscripts from authors each year. Only a few manuscripts become books. Publishers must be sure that a manuscript will sell many copies. As a result, publishers reject most of the manuscripts they receive.

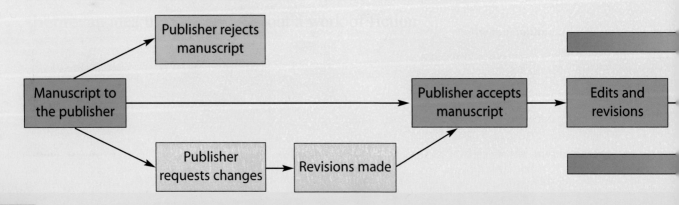

Joanne's sister, Di, was the first person with whom Joanne shared her story. Di liked Harry Potter and encouraged her sister to continue writing. Joanne applied for a writing **grant** through the Scottish Arts Council. They awarded her some money, which allowed her to finish writing the book.

In 1995, Joanne finished her novel. She bought an old typewriter and prepared several manuscripts. Now, Joanne needed an agent to help sell her work to a publishing company. She sent the first three chapters of her book to an agent. This agent rejected Joanne's idea. The second agent Joanne contacted was more interested. His name was Christopher Little. He wanted to read the rest of Joanne's manuscript.

Together, Joanne and Christopher searched for a company to publish Harry Potter. In August 1996, Christopher phoned Joanne to tell her that Bloomsbury Publishing would publish her book. After many years of work, Harry Potter would finally be published.

Inspired to Write

Joanne's favorite place to write is a café. She likes to sip coffee and have people around while she works. If she needs a break, Joanne will walk to the next coffee shop. She chooses cafés that do not play loud music. That is the only noise that disturbs her when she is writing.

Once a manuscript has been accepted, it goes through many stages before it is published. Often, authors change their work to follow an editor's suggestions. Once the book is published, some authors receive royalties. This is money based on book sales.

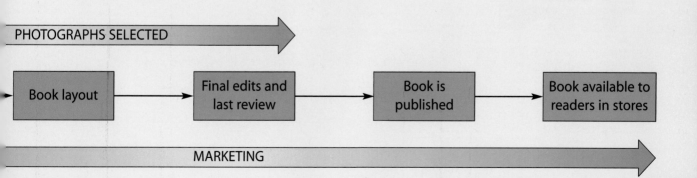

PHOTOGRAPHS SELECTED →

Book layout → Final edits and last review → Book is published → Book available to readers in stores

MARKETING →

Writer Today

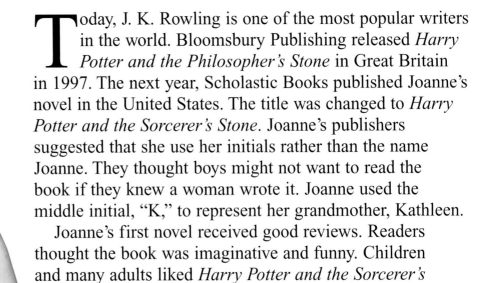

Today, J. K. Rowling is one of the most popular writers in the world. Bloomsbury Publishing released *Harry Potter and the Philosopher's Stone* in Great Britain in 1997. The next year, Scholastic Books published Joanne's novel in the United States. The title was changed to *Harry Potter and the Sorcerer's Stone*. Joanne's publishers suggested that she use her initials rather than the name Joanne. They thought boys might not want to read the book if they knew a woman wrote it. Joanne used the middle initial, "K," to represent her grandmother, Kathleen.

Joanne's first novel received good reviews. Readers thought the book was imaginative and funny. Children and many adults liked *Harry Potter and the Sorcerer's Stone*. They enjoyed reading about Harry, Ron, and Hermione, and their adventures at Hogwarts School.

With the success of her first book, Joanne's life improved. She bought a computer and used it to finish her second book, *Harry Potter and the Chamber of Secrets*.

By the time Joanne finished her fourth Harry Potter book, she was a superstar. *Harry Potter and the Goblet of Fire* became the fastest-selling book in history. It was as long as her first three novels together. Readers loved it. The fifth book, *Harry Potter and the Order of the Phoenix*, was even longer—more than 700 pages.

Joanne attended the premiere of the movie, *Harry Potter and the Prisoner of Azkaban*, in London, England, on May 30, 2004.

When the first Harry Potter books were made into movies, Joanne was concerned that the films might not be faithful to the books. Fortunately, she worked closely with the filmmakers. The movies, like the books, have been incredibly successful.

Joanne loves writing. Her books have been published all over the world. She still lives in Scotland with her family. In December 2001, she married Dr. Neil Murray. Their son, David, was born in March 2003. Joanne wrote the sixth book in the Harry Potter series, *Harry Potter and the Half-Blood Prince*, while pregnant with her third child, daughter Mackenzie.

In 1999, Joanne toured the United States, signing copies of her books for fans.

Popular Books

Although J. K. Rowling has written all her life, only the Harry Potter books have been published. Joanne has planned seven novels for the series. Each book tells about Harry's experiences during 1 year at Hogwarts School.

Harry Potter and the Sorcerer's Stone

Joanne's first book was published in the United Kingdom as *Harry Potter and the Philosopher's Stone*. In it, readers are introduced to the magical world of Harry Potter. Harry is 11 years old. He is an orphan living with his unloving relatives, the Dursleys.

One day, Harry receives a letter inviting him to attend Hogwarts School of Witchcraft and Wizardry. The letter changes his world forever. Harry discovers that his parents were wizards and that he has magical powers.

At Hogwarts School, Harry learns how to use his magical powers. He especially enjoys Quidditch, a sport played on broomsticks. Harry learns that a special jewel called the Sorcerer's Stone is hidden in Hogwarts School. The stone can give wealth and eternal life to the owner. Harry and his friends must perform daring feats to find the stone.

AWARDS
Harry Potter and the Sorcerer's Stone

1997 Nestle Smarties Prize

1997 National Book Award (UK)

1998 British Children's Book Award

1998 Publishers Weekly Best Book

1998 New York Public Library Best Book of the Year

1998 Parenting Book of the Year

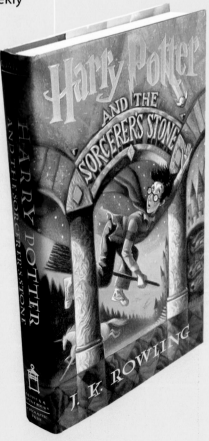

Harry Potter and the Chamber of Secrets

At the beginning of this book, Dobby, a house elf, visits Harry. Dobby warns that Harry is in danger and should not return to Hogwarts School. Harry decides to return to school anyway. When Harry and his friend, Ron, try to board the train to Hogwarts, they are unable to enter the magic train platform. The two friends must fly in a magic car to get to school.

At Hogwarts, the students have a new professor, Gilderoy Lockhart. He is vain and boastful. He is also a constant annoyance to Harry.

Strange things begin to happen at Hogwarts. A threatening message is written on a school wall. Students mysteriously turn to stone. People become suspicious of Harry when they learn he has the ability to speak to snakes. Things become more serious when Ron's sister, Ginny, is kidnapped. Harry, Ron, and Hermione are determined to solve the mystery. Together they search for a secret chamber hidden in the castle. Inside the chamber, they must face terrible dangers and bring Ginny back to safety.

AWARDS
Harry Potter and the Chamber of Secrets

1998 Nestle Smarties Prize
1999 British Children's Book Award

Harry Potter and the Prisoner of Azkaban

The wizarding world is shocked when a dangerous murderer escapes from Azkaban Prison. Sirius Black, a dark wizard, is on the loose. Now in his third year at Hogwarts School, Harry Potter's life is in danger. When Harry was a baby, Black helped Lord Voldemort kill Harry's parents. Now, Harry fears that Black will find him and murder him, too.

Frightening monsters called dementors are stationed around Hogwarts to guard the school. The dementors are so frightening that Harry faints whenever one comes near. Harry's new Defense Against Dark Arts teacher, Professor Lupin, helps him overcome his fears and unlock the secrets of his past. Hogwarts School is on high alert when an unseen intruder enters the castle. Eventually Harry, Ron, and Hermione must face the escaped wizard.

AWARDS
Harry Potter and the Prisoner of Azkaban

1999 Nestle Smarties Prize

1999 Whitbread Children's Book of the Year Award

1999 Bram Stoker Award

2000 Locus Poll Award

Harry Potter and the Goblet of Fire

When Harry returns for his fourth year at Hogwarts, the school is full of excitement. Hogwarts will host an international event called the Triwizard Tournament. Three students will compete in the tournament. One champion will be from Hogwarts, and two others will come from rival schools. Only students over the age of 17 are allowed to enter by putting their names in the "Goblet of Fire."

On Halloween night, the Goblet spits out the names of the three champions who will compete in the tournament. Everyone is shocked when the Goblet spits out a fourth name—Harry Potter. Harry is too young and does not want to compete, but the Goblet's decision is final. Few people believe Harry when he tells them he did not put his name in the Goblet. Others fear that someone is trying to harm Harry by forcing him to complete the dangerous tasks of the Triwizard Tournament. Aside from the tournament, Harry must face an even more dangerous threat—Lord Voldemort.

Harry Potter and the Order of the Phoenix

Evil Lord Voldemort has returned to the wizarding world. Harry Potter knows that Voldemort is a terrible threat, but few people believe Harry. The Ministry of Magic thinks that Harry is making up stories. Still, a group of wizards believe Harry. They form the Order of the Phoenix to fight Voldemort.

At Hogwarts School, Professor Dumbledore, the headmaster, is no longer in charge. The Ministry of Magic has sent an official to take control of the school. Delores Umbridge is the new High Inquisitor of Hogwarts. She is also Harry's teacher. Umbridge dislikes Harry because she believes Harry tells lies about Lord Voldemort.

Umbridge's punishments, year-end exams, and terrifying nightmares all make Harry's fifth year especially difficult. Harry and his friends must work together. They form a club and learn how to protect themselves from dark magic. Soon, they must confront Lord Voldemort and his evil servants.

AWARDS
Harry Potter and the Goblet of Fire
2001 Hugo Award
2001 W. H. Smith Children's Book of the Year Award

AWARDS
Harry Potter and the Order of the Phoenix
2003 Bram Stoker Award

Creative Writing Tips

Writing is difficult, but it can be very rewarding. J. K. Rowling has been working at her craft for many years. During that time, she has learned ways to make her writing better. Here are some tips that might help you write better.

Take Inspiration from Real Life

The Harry Potter books are works of fantasy, but many of the characters and ideas come from Joanne's life. Some characters have been inspired by friends or teachers Joanne knew as a girl. Are there any people, places, or situations in your life that might make a good story? You can base your writing on something real, and then add fictional ideas to it. By working your own magic, you can take real life and turn it into a great story.

Plan an Outline

Planning an outline can make writing much easier. Joanne always knows what will happen in one of her books before she sits down to write it. During the time Joanne wrote the first Harry Potter book, she was also planning the next six books in the series. After you plan your outline, think about the characters in your story.

Practice

Writing takes a great deal of practice. Joanne had to practice writing for many years before she became a successful author. She wrote many stories that were never published. Try to make time to write each day. It is also important to read as much as you can. Reading the work of successful writers will give you ideas to improve your own writing.

Use Your Imagination and Have Fun

Joanne writes the kinds of stories she would like to read. She is a writer because it is the job that gives her the greatest enjoyment. Writing is hard work, but it should also be fun. Joanne creates characters and situations that are funny, silly, and outrageous. Fans of Harry Potter will remember when he accidentally blew up his nasty Aunt Marge. Remember when Hermione's potion backfired and turned her into a cat? Follow Joanne's example, and let your imagination run wild. You can write about things that are silly or totally unrealistic.

Inspired to Write

J. K. Rowling has fun with language. You can see this in some of the names she invents. The words "Quidditch" and "Muggle" are made up. "Dumbledore" is an old English word for bumblebee. One character is named Draco Malfoy. His last name means "bad faith" in French. "Voldemort" also comes from the French language. It means "flight of death."

In the Harry Potter books and movies, Hermione uses her wand to light dark areas, open doors, and fix Harry's glasses. All of these ideas came from Joanne's imagination.

Writing a Biography Review

A biography is an account of an individual's life that is written by another person. Some people's lives are very interesting. In school, you may be asked to write a biography review. The first thing to do when writing a biography review is to decide whom you would like to learn about. Your school library or community library will have a large selection of biographies from which to choose.

Are you interested in an author, a sports figure, an inventor, a movie star, or a president? Finding the right book is your first task. Whether you choose to write your review on a biography of J. K. Rowling or another person, the task will be similar.

Begin your review by writing the title of the book, the author, and the person featured in the book. Then, start writing about the main events in the person's life. Include such things as where the person grew up and what his or her childhood was like. You will want to add details about the person's adult life, such as whether he or she married or had children. Next, write about what you think makes this person special. What kinds of experiences influenced this individual? For instance, did he or she grow up in unusual circumstances? Was the person determined to accomplish a goal? Include any details that surprised you.

A concept web is a useful research tool. Use the concept web on the right to begin researching your biography review.

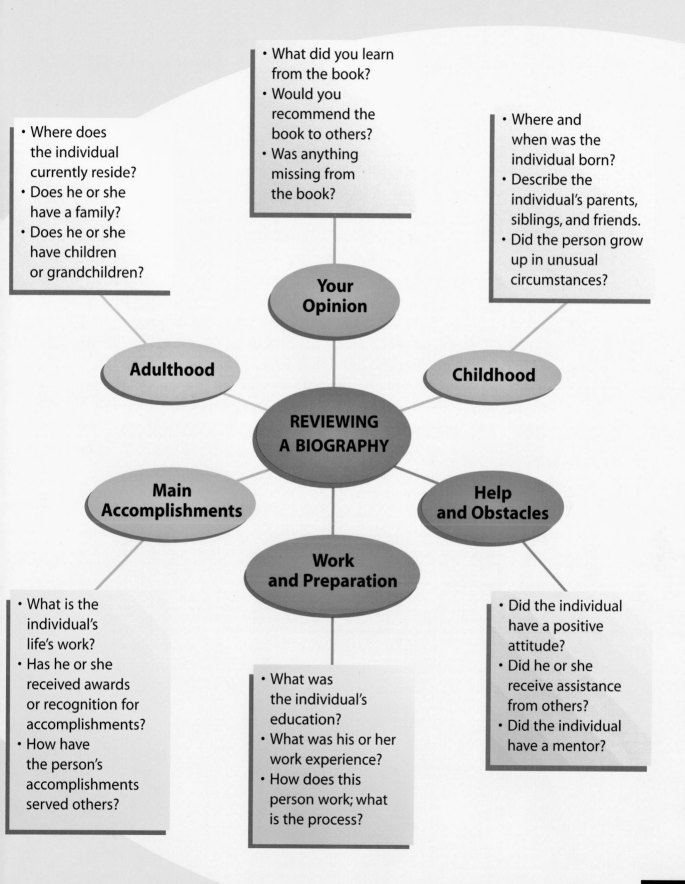

- Where does the individual currently reside?
- Does he or she have a family?
- Does he or she have children or grandchildren?

- What did you learn from the book?
- Would you recommend the book to others?
- Was anything missing from the book?

- Where and when was the individual born?
- Describe the individual's parents, siblings, and friends.
- Did the person grow up in unusual circumstances?

Your Opinion

Adulthood

Childhood

REVIEWING A BIOGRAPHY

Main Accomplishments

Help and Obstacles

Work and Preparation

- What is the individual's life's work?
- Has he or she received awards or recognition for accomplishments?
- How have the person's accomplishments served others?

- What was the individual's education?
- What was his or her work experience?
- How does this person work; what is the process?

- Did the individual have a positive attitude?
- Did he or she receive assistance from others?
- Did the individual have a mentor?

Fan Information

Readers all over the world love J. K. Rowling's books. Joanne loves to hear from her fans. Unfortunately, she receives so many letters that she cannot respond to them all. If she did, she would never have time to write.

Joanne enjoys making public appearances to read from her books. When the first Harry Potter book was released, Joanne read to small gatherings of just a few people. Today, a J. K. Rowling reading is a major event. Joanne reads to thousands of people all at once. At the SkyDome in Toronto, Canada, Joanne read to more than 20,000 people. It is thought to be the world's largest book reading.

Another special reading took place in 2003. Joanne appeared before 4,000 fans at London's Royal Albert Hall. For this event, the hall was turned into Hogwarts School. There were moving portraits and ushers dressed as Hogwarts pupils. It is a sign that she has touched many people's lives with Harry Potter's magic. Huge events like these can make Joanne nervous, but she is getting used to stardom.

Joanne enjoys meeting her fans. On June 26, 2003, she read from *Harry Potter and the Order of the Phoenix* at Royal Albert Hall in London, England.

The Internet has thousands of Web sites devoted to J. K. Rowling and Harry Potter. Some of these are official sites created by publishers, movie studios, or Joanne herself. Other sites have been created by fans who want to share information about the books and connect with other readers. You may also find interviews with Joanne or news stories about Harry Potter events.

WEB LINKS

J. K. Rowling Official Site—Harry Potter and More

www.jkrowling.com

Visitors to J. K. Rowling's official Web site can read about Joanne's life, get updates on her latest book, and learn Harry Potter trivia.

The Official Harry Potter Web Site

harrypotter.warnerbros.com

This is the official site of the Harry Potter movies by Warner Brothers. Visitors can view movie trailers, play games, and find out more about the actors who play Harry and his friends.

Quiz

Q: Where and when was J. K. Rowling born?

A: Joanne Rowling was born on July 31, 1965, in Chipping Sodbury, Great Britain.

1

2

Q: What was Joanne's favorite book when she was a child?

A: *The Little White Horse* by Elizabeth Goudge

3

Q: What subjects did Joanne study at the University of Exeter?

A: French and Classics

Q: Where was Joanne when she imagined Harry Potter?

A: On a train trip from Manchester to London

Q: What country did Joanne move to after the death of her mother?

A: Portugal

Q: Will Joanne continue to write Harry Potter books?

A: No. Joanne will only write seven books in the series.

Q: Where is Joanne's favorite place to write?

A: A café

Q: What was *Harry Potter and the Sorcerer's Stone* called in the United Kingdom?

A: *Harry Potter and the Philosopher's Stone*

Q: Where was Joanne's largest book reading?

A: The Toronto SkyDome

Q: What are the names of Harry Potter's two best friends?

A: Ron Weasley and Hermione Granger

Writing Terms

This glossary will introduce you to some of the main terms in the field of writing. Understanding these common writing terms will allow you to discuss your ideas about books and writing with others.

action: the moving events of a work of fiction

antagonist: the person in the story who opposes the main character

autobiography: a history of a person's life written by that person

biography: a written account of another person's life

character: a person in a story, poem, or play

climax: the most exciting moment or turning point in a story

episode: a short piece of action, or scene, in a story

fiction: stories about characters and events that are not real

foreshadow: hinting at something that is going to happen later in the book

imagery: a written description of a thing or idea that brings an image to mind

narrator: the speaker of the story who relates the events

nonfiction: writing that deals with real people and events

novel: published writing of considerable length that portrays characters within a story

plot: the order of events in a work of fiction

protagonist: the leading character of a story; often a likable character

resolution: the end of the story, when the conflict is settled

scene: a single episode in a story

setting: the place and time in which a work of fiction occurs

theme: an idea that runs throughout a work of fiction

Glossary

agent: a person who works with an author to help get his or her books published

central nervous system: the brain and spinal cord

Classics: literature of lasting significance

clerical: office work, such as filing and typing

grant: money awarded for a specific reason or cause

head girl: a senior student who has special responsibilities

human rights: the basic freedoms to which all people are entitled, such as the right to food and shelter, freedom from slavery, and freedom to worship

journalist: a writer who works for a newspaper or magazine

lab technician: a person who analyzes chemical samples

manuscript: draft of a story before it is published

measles: a childhood disease that causes a fever and a rash of red spots on the body

paralysis: the loss of movement or feeling in part of the body

remission: a period when a disease improves or stops progressing

scenarios: imagined sequences of possible events

settings: the places and times in which works of fiction occur

vain: too proud of one's looks, abilities, or achievements

welfare: money given by the government to help people living in poverty

Index

Photo Credits